Courageous Compassion: Navigating Cancer as a Father.

DNT Publishing

Published by DNT Publishing, 2024.

COURAGEOUS COMPASSION: NAVIGATING CANCER AS A FATHER.

First edition. January 13, 2024.

Copyright © 2024 DNT Publishing.

ISBN: 979-8224704552

Written by DNT Publishing.

Table of Contents

Introduction

Facing a cancer diagnosis, whether as a patient or a caregiver, is an emotional and challenging journey. For dads navigating this path, the experience is often layered with unique responsibilities, emotions, and considerations. This guide aims to provide support, information, and practical advice tailored to fathers who find themselves on the cancer journey.

Understanding the Diagnosis

- Deciphering Medical Terminology

- Grasping the Severity and Prognosis

The Emotional Impact on Dads

- Addressing Fear and Uncertainty

- Navigating Changes in Family Dynamics

Key Points:

- The initial emotional response to a cancer diagnosis.

- The unique challenges and fears that dads may experience.

- The importance of seeking emotional support for both the dad and the family.

Goals:

- Provide insight into the emotional rollercoaster that often accompanies a cancer diagnosis.

- Encourage open communication within the family to address fears and concerns.

- Highlight the value of seeking professional support and community resources for emotional well-being.

Understanding the Diagnosis

DECIPHERING MEDICAL Terminology

Navigating a cancer diagnosis involves grappling with a multitude of medical terms and information. In this section, we break down common cancer terminology, explaining what each term means and how it relates to the overall diagnosis. By gaining a basic understanding of the medical language, dads can feel more informed and actively participate in discussions with healthcare professionals.

Key Points:

- Explanation of common cancer-related terms.

- Understanding diagnostic tests and their significance.

- Interpreting pathology reports and imaging results.

Goals:

- Equip dads with the knowledge to comprehend and discuss medical information.

- Reduce feelings of confusion and helplessness through increased understanding.

- Empower dads to actively engage with healthcare providers in decision-making.

Grasping the Severity and Prognosis

Coming to terms with the severity of a cancer diagnosis and understanding the potential prognosis is a critical step in the journey. This section provides insights into the staging of cancer, the factors influencing prognosis, and how treatment plans are formulated. By grasping the medical aspects, dads can approach the journey with a clearer understanding of what lies ahead.

Key Points:

- Explanation of cancer staging and its implications.

- Factors influencing prognosis and treatment decisions.

- Discussions on potential treatment paths and their goals.

Goals:

- Provide a framework for comprehending the severity of the diagnosis.

- Foster realistic expectations about the journey and potential outcomes.

- Encourage open communication with healthcare providers to make informed decisions.

The Emotional Impact on Dads

Addressing Fear and Uncertainty

The emotional toll of a cancer diagnosis on dads is profound. Fear, uncertainty, and a range of emotions may surface. This section explores these feelings, providing insights into their origins and offering coping strategies. Understanding and addressing these emotions is crucial for maintaining mental well-being and supporting the family unit during this challenging time.

Key Points:

- Exploration of common fears and uncertainties dads may face.

- Identification of emotions and their impact on mental health.

- Coping strategies for managing fear and uncertainty.

Goals:

- Acknowledge and validate the emotions that may arise.

- Provide practical tools for dads to navigate and cope with fear and uncertainty.

- Encourage open communication within the family to share and address emotional challenges.

———

NAVIGATING CHANGES in Family Dynamics

A cancer diagnosis can significantly alter family dynamics. Dads may find themselves in new roles as caregivers, and children may experience a range of emotions. This section examines the shifts in family dynamics, offering guidance on maintaining healthy relationships, supporting children, and fostering open communication.

Key Points:

- Understanding the impact of the diagnosis on family roles.

- Navigating changes in parent-child relationships.

- Strategies for fostering resilience and unity within the family.

Goals:

- Provide tools for dads to adapt to changing family dynamics.

- Offer guidance on supporting children through the emotional challenges.

- Strengthen family bonds by fostering open and supportive communication.

Chapter 1: Medical Overview

Types of Cancer and Their Treatments

Understanding the specifics of the cancer diagnosis is crucial for informed decision-making. This section provides an overview of common types of cancer, their characteristics, and available treatment options. Dads will gain insights into the medical landscape, enabling them to actively engage with healthcare professionals and contribute to treatment discussions.

Key Points:

● Overview of prevalent types of cancer affecting men.

● Characteristics and variations within each type.

● An exploration of available treatment modalities.

Goals:

● Enhance dads' knowledge of the specific cancer type.

● Foster a deeper understanding of treatment options and their implications.

● Empower dads to participate actively in treatment decisions.

COMMON MEDICAL PROCEDURES and Terminology

Medical procedures and terminology can be overwhelming. This section breaks down common diagnostic procedures, treatment processes, and medical jargon. Dads will gain a clearer understanding of what to expect during medical appointments, tests, and treatment sessions, promoting a sense of control and participation in the healthcare journey.

Key Points:

- Explanation of diagnostic procedures and their purposes.

- Overview of common cancer treatments and their side effects.

- Interpretation of medical terminology encountered during the journey.

Goals:

- Reduce anxiety by demystifying medical procedures.

- Enable dads to communicate effectively with healthcare providers.

- Equip dads with the knowledge to actively engage in discussions about medical treatments.

Types of Cancer and Their Treatments

UNDERSTANDING THE SPECIFIC type of cancer is crucial for tailoring an effective treatment plan. This section provides an overview of common types of cancer that affect men, along with insights into their characteristics and treatment options.

Prostate Cancer

- Overview of prostate cancer and its prevalence.

- Screening methods and early detection.

- Treatment options, including surgery, radiation, and hormone therapy.

Lung Cancer

- Discussion on lung cancer, risk factors, and symptoms.

- Diagnostic procedures, such as imaging and biopsies.

- Treatment modalities, including surgery, chemotherapy, and targeted therapy.

Colorectal Cancer

- Introduction to colorectal cancer and its variations.

- Importance of screening and detection methods.

- Treatment approaches, including surgery, chemotherapy, and immunotherapy.

Testicular Cancer

- Overview of testicular cancer and its occurrence in young men.

- Self-examination and early detection.

- Treatment options, including surgery, chemotherapy, and surveillance.

Prostate Cancer

- Understanding pancreatic cancer and its challenges.

- Diagnostic methods, including imaging and biopsies.

- Treatment strategies, such as surgery, chemotherapy, and targeted therapy.

Blood Cancers (Leukemia, Lymphoma, and Myeloma)

- Overview of various blood cancers.

- Diagnostic procedures, including blood tests and bone marrow biopsy.

- Treatment options, such as chemotherapy, stem cell transplantation, and immunotherapy.

Skin Cancer (Melanoma and Non-Melanoma)

- Discussion on skin cancer types, risk factors, and prevention.

- Diagnosis through biopsy and imaging.

- Treatment approaches, including surgery, radiation, and immunotherapy.

Goals:

- Enhance understanding of prevalent cancer types affecting men.

- Empower dads to recognize symptoms and seek timely medical attention.

● Provide insights into various treatment modalities to facilitate informed discussions with healthcare providers.

Common Medical Procedures and Terminology

NAVIGATING THE MEDICAL landscape involves encountering various procedures and terminology. This section aims to demystify common diagnostic procedures, treatment processes, and medical terms encountered during the cancer journey.

Diagnostic Procedures

Biopsy

● Explanation of what a biopsy is and its role in cancer diagnosis.

● Overview of different biopsy types (needle biopsy, surgical biopsy) and when they are used.

● Discussion on the importance of biopsy results in determining treatment plans.

Imaging (MRI, CT Scan, PET Scan)

● Understanding different imaging techniques and their purposes.

● Overview of MRI, CT scan, and PET scan procedures.

● Explanation of how imaging helps in cancer staging and treatment planning.

Blood Tests

● Exploration of the role of blood tests in cancer diagnosis and monitoring.

● Overview of specific blood markers used in cancer detection.

● Understanding how blood tests contribute to treatment decisions.

Treatment Processes

Surgery

- Overview of surgical procedures in cancer treatment.

- Explanation of how surgery is used for tumor removal, biopsy, or reconstruction.

- Discussion on pre-operative and post-operative care.

Chemotherapy

- Understanding the basics of chemotherapy and how it targets cancer cells.

- Overview of administration methods (oral, intravenous) and treatment cycles.

- Discussion on common side effects and supportive care during chemotherapy.

Radiation Therapy

- Explanation of how radiation therapy works to destroy or damage cancer cells.

- Overview of external beam radiation and internal radiation (brachytherapy).

- Discussion on the planning and administration of radiation treatments.

Immunotherapy

- Introduction to immunotherapy and its role in cancer treatment.

- Understanding how immunotherapy harnesses the body's immune system.

- Discussion on potential side effects and ongoing research in immunotherapy.

Medical Terminology

Common Terms and Acronyms

- Compilation of frequently used medical terms and acronyms.

- Explanation of terms related to cancer staging, treatment response, and side effects.

- Quick reference guide for dads to communicate effectively with healthcare providers.

Goals:

●   Demystify common diagnostic procedures, making them more understandable for dads.

● Provide insights into different treatment processes and their purposes.

● Equip dads with a basic understanding of medical terminology for effective communication with healthcare providers.

Chapter 2: Support Systems

Cancer journeys are challenging, and having a robust support system is instrumental in navigating the complexities and uncertainties. This chapter focuses on the various support systems available to dads, providing guidance on building and utilizing these networks effectively.

Family and Friends

Open Communication

- Importance of honest and open communication within the family.

- Strategies for discussing the diagnosis with children and extended family.

- Nurturing a supportive family environment through effective communication.

Roles and Responsibilities

- Exploration of how family roles may shift during the cancer journey.

- Strategies for distributing caregiving responsibilities among family members.

- Encouraging collaboration and understanding within the family unit.

Connecting with Other Dads Going Through Similar Journeys

Support Groups and Online Communities

- Introduction to cancer support groups specifically for dads.

- Benefits of connecting with others who share similar experiences.

- Guidance on finding and participating in local or online support communities.

Shared Experiences

- Stories of resilience and inspiration from other dads on the cancer journey.

- The power of shared experiences in fostering a sense of community.

- Encouragement to seek and share support within the group.

Utilizing Professional Support Services

Counseling and Therapy

- Importance of mental health support for dads and their families.

- Overview of individual and family counseling options.

- Breaking down stigma and encouraging seeking professional help.

Palliative Care and Hospice

- Understanding the roles of palliative care and hospice in the cancer journey.

- Exploring when and how to introduce these services.

- Addressing common misconceptions about palliative and hospice care.

Goals:

- Empower dads to foster open communication within their families.

- Guide dads in navigating changing family dynamics and redistributing responsibilities.

- Highlight the value of connecting with other dads through support groups.

- Encourage utilization of professional support services for mental health and overall well-being.

Family and Friends

NAVIGATING THE CHALLENGES of a cancer journey is a collective effort that involves close collaboration with family and friends. This section delves into the importance of open communication, understanding shifting roles, and fostering a supportive environment within the family and extended social circles.

Open Communication

Honest Discussions

- The significance of open and honest discussions about the cancer diagnosis.

- Strategies for initiating conversations with family members, addressing fears, and sharing updates.

- Creating a safe space for expressing emotions and concerns within the family.

Talking to Children

- Guidance on age-appropriate discussions about cancer with children.

- Tips for reassuring and supporting children through the process.

- Resources for further assistance in explaining and addressing children's questions.

Roles and Responsibilities

Shifting Family Roles

- Understanding how family roles may evolve during the cancer journey.

- Strategies for adapting to changing responsibilities and maintaining balance.

- Encouraging open dialogue about expectations and needs within the family.

Distributing Caregiving Responsibilities

- Discussion on how to distribute caregiving responsibilities among family members.

- Recognizing the strengths and limitations of each family member.

- Promoting collaboration and mutual support in caregiving tasks.

Goals:

- Encourage open and transparent communication within the family.

- Provide guidance on discussing the cancer diagnosis with children.

- Foster an understanding of changing family dynamics and roles.

- Facilitate the equitable distribution of caregiving responsibilities.

Connecting with Other Dads Going Through Similar Journeys

FACING A CANCER DIAGNOSIS as a dad can be isolating, but connecting with others who share similar experiences can provide invaluable support. This section explores the benefits of joining support groups and online communities, sharing stories, and finding strength in collective experiences.

Support Groups and Online Communities

The Power of Shared Experiences

- Understanding the emotional benefits of connecting with others on a similar journey.

- Introduction to local and online support groups specifically for dads.

- Tips on finding and joining communities that suit individual preferences and needs.

Navigating the Dynamics of Support Groups

- Insight into the dynamics of support groups and how they function.

- Encouraging active participation and sharing within the group.

- Tips for maintaining a positive and supportive online environment.

Shared Experiences

Inspirational Stories

- Showcasing stories of resilience and inspiration from dads who have navigated similar journeys.

- The impact of shared experiences in providing hope and encouragement.

- How personal narratives can help normalize emotions and experiences.

Establishing Connections

- Strategies for building connections within the support group.

- The role of mutual support in alleviating feelings of isolation.

- Encouraging dads to share their own experiences to benefit others.

Goals:

- Highlight the emotional benefits of connecting with other dads.

- Provide guidance on finding and participating in support groups.

- Showcase inspirational stories to provide hope and encouragement.

- Encourage active engagement within support communities for mutual support.

Utilizing Professional Support Services

FACING A CANCER DIAGNOSIS involves complex emotions, and seeking professional support services can be instrumental in providing guidance and coping strategies. This section explores the importance of counseling, therapy, palliative care, and hospice services for dads and their families.

Counseling and Therapy

Individual Counseling

- Understanding the role of individual counseling in addressing personal emotions and coping mechanisms.

- Exploring the benefits of talking to a mental health professional.

- Guidance on finding a counselor experienced in supporting individuals dealing with cancer.

Family Counseling

● The significance of family counseling in fostering open communication and understanding.

● Strategies for addressing family dynamics and supporting each member.

● Encouraging families to explore counseling services together.

Palliative Care and Hospice

Introduction to Palliative Care

● Defining palliative care and its role in improving the quality of life during treatment.

● Understanding how palliative care complements traditional medical treatment.

● Tips for initiating discussions about palliative care with healthcare providers.

Hospice Care

● Clarifying the role of hospice care in end-of-life situations.

● Discussing the benefits of hospice services for both the patient and family.

● Guidance on when and how to consider hospice care as part of the overall care plan.

Goals:

● Highlight the importance of seeking professional support services.

● Provide insights into the role of individual and family counseling.

● Introduce palliative care as a holistic approach to enhance quality of life.

● Clarify the purpose and benefits of hospice care in specific situations.

Chapter 3: Coping Strategies

Coping with the challenges of a cancer journey is essential for maintaining mental and emotional well-being. This chapter focuses on practical coping strategies that dads can employ to navigate the complexities of their roles as caregivers and emotional supporters.

Managing Stress and Anxiety

Mindfulness and Relaxation Techniques

- Introduction to mindfulness practices and their stress-relieving benefits.

- Guided relaxation exercises and techniques for managing anxiety.

- Incorporating mindfulness into daily routines for sustained well-being.

Healthy Lifestyle Choices

- The impact of nutrition, exercise, and sleep on stress management.

- Strategies for incorporating healthy lifestyle choices into daily life.

- Creating a supportive environment for overall well-being.

Balancing Work and Caregiving

Open Communication with Employers

- The importance of transparent communication with employers about the caregiving role.

- Discussing potential workplace accommodations and support.

- Navigating challenges and finding a balance between work responsibilities and caregiving duties.

Time Management and Prioritization

- Strategies for effective time management to balance caregiving and personal commitments.

- Prioritizing tasks to reduce feelings of overwhelm and stress.

- Seeking external support when needed to manage responsibilities.

Taking Care of Your Own Health

Regular Health Checkups

- Emphasizing the importance of dads prioritizing their own health.

- Encouraging regular checkups and screenings for early detection.

- Addressing common health concerns and seeking timely medical attention.

Seeking Emotional Support

- Normalizing the act of seeking emotional support for dads.

- Identifying trusted friends, family members, or professionals for emotional outlets.

- Encouraging participation in support groups for shared experiences.

Goals:

- Provide practical coping strategies for managing stress and anxiety.

- Offer guidance on balancing work responsibilities with caregiving duties.

- Emphasize the importance of maintaining personal health and seeking emotional support.

Managing Stress and Anxiety

COPING WITH STRESS and anxiety is integral to maintaining well-being during the challenges of a cancer journey. This section provides practical strategies for dads to manage stress and anxiety effectively.

Mindfulness and Relaxation Techniques

Introduction to Mindfulness

● Understanding the concept of mindfulness and its benefits for stress reduction.

● Simple mindfulness exercises for dads to incorporate into their daily routines.

● Exploring the power of being present and cultivating a mindful mindset.

Guided Relaxation Exercises

● Providing step-by-step guidance on relaxation exercises.

● Deep-breathing techniques to promote relaxation and alleviate tension.

● Incorporating guided imagery for mental and emotional calmness.

Healthy Lifestyle Choices

Nutrition for Stress Management

● Exploring the connection between nutrition and stress.

● Guidelines for maintaining a balanced and nourishing diet.

● Identifying foods that contribute to stress reduction.

Exercise for Stress Relief

● Highlighting the role of physical activity in stress management.

● Incorporating exercise into daily routines, even with time constraints.

● Recognizing the benefits of movement for mental well-being.

Quality Sleep Habits

● Importance of sleep in stress reduction and overall health.

● Tips for establishing healthy sleep habits.

- Creating a conducive sleep environment for restorative rest.

Goals:

- Introduce mindfulness as a tool for stress reduction.

- Provide practical relaxation exercises for immediate stress relief.

- Offer guidance on nutrition, exercise, and sleep for overall well-being.

- Empower dads to integrate these strategies into their daily routines for sustained stress management.

Balancing Work and Caregiving

BALANCING THE DEMANDS of work with the responsibilities of caregiving during a cancer journey requires careful planning and effective communication. This section provides strategies for dads to navigate this delicate balance.

Open Communication with Employers

Initiating Transparent Conversations

- Guidance on communicating openly with employers about the caregiving role.

- Tips for discussing the cancer diagnosis and potential impact on work.

- Identifying potential workplace accommodations and support.

Establishing a Flexible Work Arrangement

- Exploring flexible work options and negotiating schedules.

- Strategies for presenting a compelling case for flexible arrangements.

- Navigating challenges and maintaining open lines of communication with employers.

Time Management and Prioritization

Creating a Caregiving Schedule

- Developing a caregiving schedule that aligns with work commitments.

- Strategies for effective time management to avoid burnout.

- Involving family members in creating a shared caregiving plan.

Setting Realistic Expectations

- Recognizing personal limitations and setting realistic expectations.

- Strategies for prioritizing tasks to manage both work and caregiving responsibilities.

- Seeking external support when needed and acknowledging the importance of self-care.

Goals:

- Empower dads to have transparent conversations with employers about their caregiving role.

- Provide guidance on negotiating flexible work arrangements.

- Offer strategies for effective time management and prioritization.

- Encourage realistic expectations and self-care to prevent burnout.

Taking Care of Your Own Health

AMIDST THE CHALLENGES of caregiving and supporting a loved one through a cancer journey, it's crucial for dads to prioritize their own health. This section provides guidance on maintaining personal well-being and seeking support when needed.

Regular Health Checkups

Importance of Regular Checkups

- Emphasizing the significance of routine health checkups for dads.

- Overview of screenings and examinations tailored to men's health.

- Strategies for incorporating regular health checkups into a busy schedule.

Early Detection and Prevention

- Understanding the role of early detection in preventing health issues.

- Encouraging proactive measures for preventive healthcare.

- Identifying potential warning signs and seeking timely medical attention.

Seeking Emotional Support

Normalizing the Act of Seeking Support

- Breaking down stigmas around seeking emotional support for dads.

- Encouraging the recognition of emotional needs and the importance of addressing them.

- Identifying trusted friends, family members, or professionals for emotional outlets.

Participation in Support Groups

- The value of joining support groups for emotional well-being.

- Building connections with other dads facing similar challenges.

- Strategies for active participation in support communities.

Goals:

- Emphasize the importance of regular health checkups for dads.

- Provide guidance on early detection and preventive measures.

- Encourage dads to normalize seeking emotional support.

- Highlight the benefits of participating in support groups for shared experiences.

Chapter 4: Communication and Advocacy

Effective communication and advocacy play a central role in navigating the complexities of a cancer journey. This chapter provides insights and strategies for dads to communicate with healthcare providers, advocate for the best care, and facilitate open discussions within the family.

Talking to Your Children About Cancer

Age-Appropriate Discussions

- Tailoring conversations about cancer based on the age of the children.

- Strategies for addressing questions and concerns in a developmentally appropriate manner.

- Creating a supportive environment for children to express their emotions.

Reinforcing Love and Support

- Emphasizing the ongoing love and support within the family.

- Providing reassurance and encouragement during the cancer journey.

- Addressing common fears and misconceptions children may have.

Effective Communication with Healthcare Providers

Establishing Open Communication

- The importance of building a collaborative relationship with healthcare providers.

- Strategies for asking questions and seeking clarification about the diagnosis and treatment plan.

- Encouraging an open dialogue to address concerns and preferences.

Keeping a Medical Journal

● Creating a comprehensive medical journal to track appointments, treatments, and symptoms.

● Facilitating communication with healthcare providers by maintaining organized records.

● Utilizing the journal to actively participate in treatment discussions.

Advocating for the Best Care for Your Loved One

Becoming an Informed Advocate

● The role of dads as advocates for their loved ones.

● Strategies for becoming informed about the diagnosis, treatment options, and potential side effects.

● Building confidence to actively engage in healthcare decisions.

Collaboration with the Healthcare Team

● The importance of collaborating with the healthcare team to optimize care.

● Strategies for effective communication with doctors, nurses, and support staff.

● Advocating for personalized care plans that align with the needs of the individual.

Goals:

● Provide guidance on age-appropriate discussions with children about cancer.

● Empower dads to establish open communication with healthcare providers.

● Encourage the use of a medical journal for organized communication.

● Foster advocacy skills to actively participate in healthcare decisions.

Talking to Your Children About Cancer

DISCUSSING A CANCER diagnosis with children is a delicate and important aspect of the cancer journey. This section provides strategies and guidance for dads in navigating age-appropriate conversations and supporting their children emotionally.

Age-Appropriate Discussions

Understanding Developmental Levels

● Insight into the different developmental stages and levels of understanding in children.

● Tailoring conversations based on the age and maturity of each child.

● Identifying appropriate language and concepts for effective communication.

Creating a Safe and Supportive Environment

● Establishing an environment where children feel safe expressing their thoughts and feelings.

● Encouraging an open-door policy for questions and concerns.

● Addressing emotions and ensuring children know their feelings are valid.

Reinforcing Love and Support

Emphasizing Continuity and Routine

● Highlighting the stability and continuity of family routines despite changes.

● Reinforcing that love and support within the family remain constant.

● Providing reassurance that the child is not responsible for the cancer.

Addressing Common Fears and Misconceptions

● Identifying and addressing common fears and misconceptions children may have.

● Offering age-appropriate explanations about the nature of cancer and its treatment.

● Correcting misunderstandings to reduce anxiety and uncertainty.

Goals:

● Provide strategies for age-appropriate discussions about cancer with children.

● Encourage the creation of a safe and supportive environment for open communication.

● Highlight the importance of reinforcing love, support, and continuity for children.

● Address common fears and misconceptions to reduce anxiety and uncertainty.

Effective Communication with Healthcare Providers

ESTABLISHING OPEN AND effective communication with healthcare providers is essential for obtaining the best care and navigating the complexities of a cancer journey. This section provides strategies for dads to communicate with healthcare teams and actively engage in the decision-making process.

Establishing Open Communication

Building a Collaborative Relationship

● The importance of building a collaborative and trusting relationship with healthcare providers.

● Strategies for fostering open communication and mutual respect.

● Creating an environment where questions and concerns are welcomed.

Asking Questions and Seeking Clarification

● Encouraging dads to ask questions about the diagnosis, treatment options, and potential side effects.

- Strategies for seeking clarification on medical terms and procedures.

- Empowering dads to be proactive in understanding and participating in the treatment plan.

Keeping a Medical Journal

Importance of Record Keeping

- Recognizing the benefits of maintaining a comprehensive medical journal.

- Logging details of appointments, treatments, medications, and symptoms.

- Enhancing communication with healthcare providers by presenting organized and accurate information.

Utilizing the Medical Journal in Discussions

- Tips for using the medical journal as a tool for communication during appointments.

- Discussing treatment responses, side effects, and any concerns recorded in the journal.

- Collaborating with healthcare providers to make informed decisions based on the documented information.

Goals:

- Empower dads to establish a collaborative relationship with healthcare providers.

- Encourage proactive questioning and seeking clarification during medical discussions.

- Highlight the benefits of keeping a medical journal for organized communication.

- Facilitate the use of the medical journal as a tool for effective discussions with healthcare providers.

Advocating for the Best Care for Your Loved One

AS A DAD NAVIGATING the challenges of a cancer journey, advocating for the best care for your loved one is a crucial role. This section provides guidance and strategies for becoming an informed advocate and actively engaging with the healthcare team.

Becoming an Informed Advocate

Understanding the Diagnosis and Treatment Options

- The importance of gaining a comprehensive understanding of the cancer diagnosis.

- Strategies for researching treatment options, potential side effects, and alternative therapies.

- Empowering dads to actively participate in informed decision-making.

Communicating Preferences and Values

- Encouraging dads to communicate personal preferences and values in the treatment plan.

- Strategies for expressing concerns, expectations, and goals for the care journey.

- Advocating for a personalized care approach that aligns with the individual's needs.

Collaboration with the Healthcare Team

Effective Communication with Healthcare Providers

- Reinforcing the importance of clear and open communication with the healthcare team.

- Strategies for actively engaging in discussions about treatment plans, side effects, and adjustments.

- Collaborating with healthcare providers to ensure a holistic and patient-centered approach.

Seeking Second Opinions

● Discussing the option of seeking second opinions for complex diagnoses or treatment plans.

● Guidance on approaching healthcare providers about the intention to seek additional perspectives.

● The role of second opinions in making informed decisions about care.

Goals:

● Empower dads to become informed advocates for their loved ones.

● Encourage communication of personal preferences and values in the treatment plan.

● Foster collaboration with the healthcare team for a patient-centered approach.

● Provide guidance on seeking second opinions when appropriate.

CHAPTER 5: FINANCIAL and Legal Considerations

Navigating the financial and legal aspects of a cancer journey is crucial for ensuring the well-being of the family. This chapter provides guidance for dads on managing financial concerns, understanding legal considerations, and accessing available resources.

Managing Financial Concerns

Understanding Insurance Coverage

● Overview of health insurance policies and their coverage.

- Guidance on reviewing insurance plans to understand benefits and limitations.

- Strategies for addressing potential gaps in coverage and exploring additional options.

Exploring Financial Assistance Programs

- Information on available financial assistance programs for medical expenses.

- Guidance on eligibility criteria and the application process for assistance.

- Connecting with local and national organizations that offer financial support.

Legal Considerations and Planning

Power of Attorney and Advanced Directives

- Explanation of power of attorney and its role in healthcare decision-making.

- Guidance on creating advanced directives to outline preferences for medical treatment.

- Strategies for discussing and documenting end-of-life wishes with family members.

Estate Planning and Will Preparation

- Overview of estate planning considerations for dads and their families.

- Guidance on the importance of creating a will to outline distribution of assets.

- Strategies for involving legal professionals in the estate planning process.

Accessing Available Resources

Local and National Support Organizations

- Compilation of local and national organizations providing financial and legal assistance.

- Guidance on connecting with community resources for additional support.

- Utilizing online platforms and directories to access available resources.

Goals:

- Provide guidance on understanding and managing health insurance coverage.

- Highlight available financial assistance programs for medical expenses.

- Offer information on legal considerations, including power of attorney and estate planning.

- Connect dads with local and national support organizations for financial and legal assistance.

Understanding Medical Costs and Insurance

NAVIGATING THE COMPLEX landscape of medical costs and insurance is a critical aspect of managing the financial aspects of a cancer journey. This section provides guidance for dads on understanding insurance coverage, managing medical expenses, and accessing financial assistance programs.

Understanding Insurance Coverage

Reviewing Health Insurance Policies

- Importance of thoroughly reviewing health insurance policies.

- Understanding the coverage limits, deductibles, co-pays, and out-of-pocket expenses.

- Strategies for contacting the insurance provider to clarify coverage details.

Addressing Coverage Gaps

- Identifying potential gaps in coverage for specific medical treatments or procedures.

- Guidance on seeking supplemental insurance or exploring alternative coverage options.

- Strategies for proactively addressing coverage limitations and potential out-of-pocket expenses.

Managing Medical Expenses

Budgeting and Financial Planning

- Developing a budget and financial plan to manage medical expenses.

- Strategies for prioritizing expenses and identifying areas for potential cost savings.

- Seeking financial counseling or assistance to create a realistic financial plan.

Negotiating Medical Bills

- Guidance on negotiating medical bills with healthcare providers.

- Exploring the option of setting up payment plans or arranging for financial assistance.

- Tips for communicating openly with billing departments to address financial concerns.

EXPLORING FINANCIAL Assistance Programs

Researching Available Assistance Programs

- Overview of local and national financial assistance programs for medical expenses.

- Guidance on researching eligibility criteria and application processes.

- Utilizing online resources and community organizations to access financial support.

Goals:

- Empower dads to understand their health insurance policies thoroughly.

● Provide strategies for addressing potential gaps in coverage.

● Offer guidance on budgeting and financial planning for managing medical expenses.

● Highlight available financial assistance programs and resources for additional support.

Legal Matters and Planning

ADDRESSING LEGAL MATTERS and planning is essential for dads navigating a cancer journey. This section provides guidance on crucial legal considerations, including power of attorney, advanced directives, and estate planning.

Power of Attorney and Advanced Directives

Understanding Power of Attorney

● Explanation of power of attorney and its role in healthcare decision-making.

● Guidance on selecting a trusted individual to act as a healthcare proxy.

● Strategies for discussing and documenting preferences for medical treatment.

Creating Advanced Directives

● Importance of creating advanced directives to outline medical treatment preferences.

● Overview of the types of decisions covered by advanced directives.

● Guidance on involving family members and healthcare providers in the creation of advanced directives.

Estate Planning and Will Preparation

Overview of Estate Planning

● Understanding the significance of estate planning for dads and their families.

- Guidance on determining the distribution of assets and property.

- Strategies for involving legal professionals in the estate planning process.

Importance of Creating a Will

- Explanation of the importance of creating a will.

- Overview of the components typically included in a comprehensive will.

- Strategies for regularly updating and reviewing the will as circumstances change.

Goals:

- Provide guidance on understanding and establishing power of attorney.

- Encourage the creation of advanced directives to outline medical treatment preferences.

- Emphasize the importance of estate planning for the well-being of the family.

- Highlight the significance of creating and regularly updating a comprehensive will.

Chapter 6: Practical Tips for Daily Life

Balancing the demands of daily life while navigating a cancer journey requires practical strategies. This chapter provides dads with actionable tips for managing daily tasks, maintaining a supportive home environment, and fostering well-being.

Organizing Daily Tasks

Creating a Practical Schedule

● Developing a daily schedule that accommodates both caregiving responsibilities and personal tasks.

● Strategies for prioritizing and organizing tasks to maximize efficiency.

● Incorporating flexibility to adapt to changing circumstances.

Delegating and Seeking Support

● The importance of delegating tasks to family members and friends.

● Strategies for effectively communicating and distributing responsibilities.

● Utilizing support networks to share the caregiving load.

Maintaining a Supportive Home Environment

Creating a Comfortable Space

● Tips for creating a comfortable and calming environment at home.

● Incorporating elements that contribute to a positive and supportive atmosphere.

● Addressing practical considerations for a functional and accessible living space.

Nurturing Emotional Well-Being

- Fostering open communication within the family.

- Encouraging regular family meetings to address concerns and share updates.

- Identifying and implementing activities that promote emotional well-being for all family members.

Self-Care Strategies for Dads

Prioritizing Personal Well-Being

- Emphasizing the importance of self-care for dads.

- Strategies for incorporating self-care activities into daily routines.

- Encouraging regular breaks and moments of relaxation.

Connecting with Support Networks

- The value of connecting with other dads facing similar challenges.

- Strategies for actively participating in support groups and online communities.

- Building a reliable network of friends and family for emotional support.

Goals:

- Provide practical tips for organizing daily tasks and responsibilities.

- Guide dads in creating a supportive home environment.

- Emphasize the importance of self-care and well-being.

- Encourage active participation in support networks for emotional support.

Creating a Comfortable Living Space

ENSURING A COMFORTABLE and supportive living space is crucial for both the individual facing cancer and their family. This section provides practical tips for dads on creating a home environment that fosters well-being and facilitates the challenges of the cancer journey.

Prioritizing Practical Considerations

Accessibility and Functionality

- Assessing the home for accessibility and making necessary adjustments.

- Creating a functional layout that accommodates any mobility challenges.

- Identifying and addressing potential safety concerns within the living space.

Comfortable Seating and Rest Areas

- Choosing comfortable and supportive furniture, especially for long periods of rest.

- Creating cozy and inviting rest areas within the home.

- Utilizing cushions, blankets, and other items for added comfort.

Enhancing the Atmosphere

Personalized Decor and Belongings

- Incorporating personal touches and familiar belongings into the living space.

- Displaying cherished items, photographs, and artwork to create a comforting atmosphere.

- Ensuring that the individual facing cancer feels a sense of familiarity and connection.

Natural Light and Ventilation

- Maximizing natural light to create a bright and uplifting environment.

- Ensuring proper ventilation for a fresh and comfortable living space.

- Arranging furniture to optimize the benefits of natural light and airflow.

Emotional Support Spaces

Creating Relaxation Zones

- Designating specific areas for relaxation and stress relief.

- Incorporating elements such as comfortable seating, calming colors, and soft lighting.

- Encouraging moments of quiet reflection and relaxation.

Open Communication Spaces

- Arranging spaces that facilitate open communication within the family.

- Creating a central area for family meetings and discussions.

- Ensuring that the living space accommodates the emotional needs of everyone in the family.

Goals:

- Provide guidance on making practical adjustments for accessibility.

- Offer tips for choosing comfortable furniture and creating restful areas.

- Emphasize the importance of personalizing the living space with familiar belongings.

- Encourage the creation of spaces that support relaxation, open communication, and emotional well-being.

Meal Planning and Nutrition

MAINTAINING A BALANCED and nutritious diet is crucial during a cancer journey, supporting the overall well-being of both the individual facing cancer and their family. This section provides practical tips for dads on meal planning and nutrition.

Creating a Nutrient-Rich Meal Plan

Balanced Meal Composition

- Guidance on crafting meals that include a variety of food groups for balanced nutrition.

● Incorporating fruits, vegetables, lean proteins, whole grains, and dairy into daily meals.

● Working with healthcare providers or nutritionists to tailor the meal plan to specific dietary needs.

Small, Frequent Meals

● Considering the benefits of smaller, more frequent meals throughout the day.

● Providing a steady source of energy and nutrients to support overall well-being.

● Planning convenient and nutritious snacks for in-between meals.

Practical Meal Preparation Tips

Batch Cooking and Freezing

● Streamlining meal preparation by cooking in batches and freezing portions.

● Ensuring a variety of nutritious options are readily available, even on busy days.

● Labeling and organizing frozen meals for easy retrieval.

Collaborative Meal Preparation

● Involving family members in meal preparation to share responsibilities.

● Turning meal preparation into a bonding activity for the family.

● Encouraging creativity and flexibility in adapting recipes to suit individual preferences.

Addressing Specific Dietary Needs

Consulting Healthcare Professionals

● Seeking guidance from healthcare professionals or nutritionists to address specific dietary needs.

- Adapting meal plans to accommodate any dietary restrictions or preferences.

- Understanding the role of nutrition in managing side effects of treatments.

Hydration Considerations

- Emphasizing the importance of staying hydrated during the cancer journey.

- Providing tips for incorporating hydrating foods and beverages into daily routines.

- Monitoring and adjusting fluid intake based on individual needs.

Goals:

- Provide guidance on creating a nutrient-rich and balanced meal plan.

- Offer practical tips for meal preparation, including batch cooking and collaborative efforts.

- Address the importance of adapting meal plans to specific dietary needs.

- Emphasize hydration considerations for overall well-being.

Balancing Responsibilities

BALANCING THE VARIOUS responsibilities that come with being a dad and a caregiver during a cancer journey is challenging but essential for overall well-being. This section provides practical tips for dads on effectively managing and balancing their responsibilities.

Prioritizing and Organizing Tasks

Establishing Priorities

- Identifying and prioritizing tasks based on urgency and importance.

- Focusing on essential responsibilities while recognizing less critical tasks.

- Setting realistic expectations for what can be achieved within a given timeframe.

Creating a Task Schedule

● Developing a daily or weekly schedule that allocates time for specific responsibilities.

● Utilizing tools such as calendars or task management apps to stay organized.

● Adjusting schedules as needed to accommodate unexpected challenges.

Delegating and Seeking Support

Sharing Responsibilities with Family

● Communicating openly with family members about the caregiving role.

● Delegating tasks and responsibilities to distribute the workload.

● Encouraging family members to actively participate in caregiving responsibilities.

Seeking External Support

● Identifying external support networks, such as friends or community resources.

● Communicating needs and seeking assistance when overwhelmed.

● Understanding that seeking help is a sign of strength and responsible caregiving.

PRACTICING SELF-CARE

Allocating Time for Self-Care

● Recognizing the importance of self-care in maintaining physical and mental well-being.

● Allocating dedicated time for personal activities, hobbies, and relaxation.

● Communicating the need for self-care to family members and seeking their understanding.

Connecting with Support Groups

- Engaging with support groups for caregivers to share experiences and tips.

- Building connections with other dads facing similar challenges.

- Learning from the experiences of others and gaining insights into effective strategies.

Goals:

- Provide practical tips for prioritizing and organizing tasks.

- Encourage the delegation of responsibilities within the family.

- Highlight the importance of seeking external support when needed.

- Emphasize the practice of self-care for overall well-being.

Chapter 7: Hope and Resilience

Maintaining hope and resilience is crucial for dads navigating the challenges of a cancer journey. This chapter provides insights, strategies, and inspirational guidance to foster a sense of hope and resilience during difficult times.

Nurturing Hope

Cultivating a Positive Mindset

● Encouraging dads to focus on positive aspects and maintain an optimistic outlook.

● Strategies for finding hope in small victories and moments of joy.

● Building resilience through the power of positive thinking.

Setting Realistic Expectations

● Guidance on setting achievable goals and expectations for the journey.

● Recognizing that setbacks are a natural part of the process.

● Emphasizing the importance of adapting expectations based on the current circumstances.

Building Resilience

Embracing Adaptability

● Fostering the ability to adapt to changing circumstances.

● Strategies for adjusting to new challenges and uncertainties.

● Recognizing that resilience is strengthened through flexibility and adaptability.

Seeking Support and Connection

- Encouraging dads to lean on their support networks during challenging times.

- Building resilience through shared experiences and connections.

- Recognizing the strength that comes from seeking and accepting support.

Finding Meaning and Purpose

Identifying Personal Values and Goals

- Reflecting on personal values and goals to find meaning in the journey.

- Connecting daily actions with a sense of purpose and fulfillment.

- Embracing the journey as an opportunity for personal growth and learning.

Celebrating Moments of Joy and Achievement

- Acknowledging and celebrating moments of joy and accomplishment.

- Creating positive rituals and traditions to mark important milestones.

- Recognizing the resilience that comes from finding joy in challenging times.

Inspirational Stories and Quotes

Sharing Stories of Hope and Resilience

- Showcasing inspirational stories of individuals who have navigated similar journeys.

- Highlighting the strength and resilience displayed in challenging circumstances.

- Providing a source of inspiration for dads facing the uncertainties of the cancer journey.

Goals:

- Provide insights on cultivating hope and maintaining a positive mindset.

● Offer strategies for building resilience in the face of challenges.

● Encourage the identification of personal values and goals for a sense of purpose.

● Share inspirational stories and quotes to uplift and inspire during difficult times.

Stories of Inspiration

IN TIMES OF CHALLENGE, stories of hope and resilience can serve as powerful sources of inspiration. Here are a few uplifting narratives from individuals who have navigated the complexities of a cancer journey:

A Father's Determination

Mark, a devoted father, faced the news of his child's cancer diagnosis with unwavering determination. Despite the emotional turmoil, he channeled his energy into researching treatment options, connecting with support groups, and fostering a positive environment at home. Mark's resilience and proactive approach not only supported his child through treatment but also inspired other dads facing similar challenges.

The Strength of Community

In a tight-knit community, Jason found strength and solace when his wife was diagnosed with cancer. Friends, neighbors, and fellow parents rallied together to provide meals, offer childcare, and lend emotional support. The collective resilience of the community became a beacon of hope, demonstrating the profound impact of shared compassion during difficult times.

Turning Adversity into Advocacy

Facing his own cancer diagnosis, Tom transformed adversity into advocacy. Determined to raise awareness, he became an active participant in cancer-related organizations, sharing his journey to inspire others. Tom's commitment to making a positive impact showcased the resilience that can arise when individuals find purpose beyond their personal struggles.

A Family's Creative Coping

The Johnson family, dealing with the challenges of cancer treatment for their child, discovered the therapeutic power of creativity. They embraced art, music, and storytelling as outlets for expression and healing. The family's ability to find joy and connection through creative endeavors became a testament to resilience and the transformative nature of positive outlets.

Embracing Moments of Joy

Sarah, a mother facing her own cancer journey, focused on creating moments of joy for her family. From simple activities like picnics in the backyard to celebrating small achievements, she emphasized the importance of cherishing positive moments amidst the difficulties. Sarah's approach illustrated how finding joy can contribute to resilience and the overall well-being of the family.

Goals:

● Share real-life stories of individuals who found inspiration and resilience during a cancer journey.

● Illustrate the diverse ways people cope, find strength, and maintain hope.

● Provide examples of how individuals turn adversity into advocacy and support.

Finding Meaning in the Journey

NAVIGATING A CANCER journey can be an opportunity for personal growth, introspection, and finding meaning. This section explores ways in which dads can identify personal values, set meaningful goals, and discover purpose amidst the challenges.

Reflecting on Personal Values and Goals

Journaling and Self-Reflection

● Encouraging dads to engage in journaling and self-reflection.

● Identifying and articulating personal values that guide decision-making.

- Reflecting on individual goals and aspirations, both personal and familial.

Family Values Discussion

- Facilitating open discussions with the family about shared values.

- Collaboratively identifying values that unite the family and contribute to a supportive environment.

- Using these values as a foundation for decision-making during the journey.

Connecting Daily Actions with Purpose

Aligning Actions with Values

- Empowering dads to align their daily actions with identified values.

- Making intentional choices that resonate with personal and family values.

- Recognizing the impact of small, purposeful actions on overall well-being.

Setting Purposeful Intentions

- Setting daily intentions that contribute to a sense of purpose.

- Acknowledging and celebrating moments when actions align with intentions.

- Embracing the journey as an opportunity for intentional living.

Embracing the Journey as an Opportunity for Growth

Emphasizing Personal Growth

- Viewing the challenges of the cancer journey as opportunities for personal growth.

- Recognizing strengths and capabilities that may emerge during difficult times.

- Encouraging a mindset that embraces learning and development.

Supporting Family Growth

● Fostering an environment that supports the growth and development of each family member.

● Encouraging open communication about individual and collective aspirations.

● Nurturing resilience and adaptability as essential components of family growth.

Goals:

● Guide dads in reflecting on personal values and setting meaningful goals.

● Encourage open family discussions about shared values.

● Empower dads to align daily actions with a sense of purpose.

● Foster a mindset that views the cancer journey as an opportunity for personal and family growth.

Chapter 8: End-of-Life Considerations

Addressing end-of-life considerations is a sensitive but important aspect of the cancer journey. This chapter provides guidance for dads on navigating end-of-life discussions, making informed decisions, and providing support during this challenging phase.

Open and Honest Communication

Initiating End-of-Life Discussions

● Understanding the importance of open and honest communication about end-of-life preferences.

● Strategies for initiating conversations with the individual facing cancer and family members.

● Creating a supportive and compassionate environment for discussing wishes and concerns.

Honoring Individual Choices

● Respecting the autonomy of the individual facing cancer in expressing their preferences.

● Discussing specific medical interventions, quality of life, and personal values.

● Encouraging ongoing communication to address evolving preferences.

Making Informed Decisions

Advance Care Planning

● Explaining the concept of advance care planning and its role in decision-making.

● Guidance on documenting preferences regarding medical treatments and interventions.

● Involving healthcare professionals in discussions about advance directives.

Palliative and Hospice Care

● Providing information on the benefits of palliative and hospice care.

● Understanding the differences between palliative care and curative treatments.

● Collaborating with healthcare providers to determine the most appropriate care plan.

Emotional and Spiritual Support

Nurturing Emotional Well-Being

● Recognizing and addressing the emotional impact of end-of-life discussions on the family.

● Encouraging open expression of feelings, fears, and concerns.

● Utilizing the support of counselors, therapists, or spiritual advisors.

Spiritual Considerations

● Addressing spiritual beliefs and practices during the end-of-life phase.

● Providing opportunities for spiritual connection, rituals, and discussions.

● Respecting diverse spiritual perspectives within the family.

PRACTICAL CONSIDERATIONS and Arrangements

Legal and Financial Matters

● Reviewing legal considerations, including wills, power of attorney, and estate planning.

● Seeking legal advice to ensure all necessary documents are in place.

● Discussing financial matters and identifying available resources for end-of-life care.

Practical Arrangements

● Making practical arrangements, such as funeral planning and memorial preferences.

● Involving family members in discussions about end-of-life logistics.

● Ensuring that practical matters are addressed with sensitivity and care.

Goals:

● Guide dads in initiating open and honest end-of-life discussions.

● Encourage the documentation of preferences through advance care planning.

● Provide information on palliative and hospice care options.

● Support emotional well-being and spiritual considerations during this challenging phase.

● Address practical matters and legal considerations with sensitivity and compassion.

Hospice and Palliative Care

UNDERSTANDING AND CONSIDERING hospice and palliative care options is a crucial aspect of end-of-life considerations. This section provides information for dads on the roles of hospice and palliative care, helping them make informed decisions aligned with the individual's preferences.

Palliative Care: Enhancing Quality of Life

Definition and Purpose

● Defining palliative care as specialized medical care focused on relieving symptoms and improving quality of life.

- Highlighting the multidisciplinary approach that addresses physical, emotional, and spiritual needs.

- Emphasizing that palliative care can be provided alongside curative treatments.

When to Consider Palliative Care

- Recognizing the benefits of early integration of palliative care, not limited to the end-of-life stage.

- Discussing the transition to palliative care when the focus shifts from curative treatments to symptom management.

- Understanding that palliative care can be provided at home, in hospitals, or specialized care facilities.

Hospice Care: Comfort and Support in End-of-Life

Overview and Goals

- Defining hospice care as compassionate end-of-life care focused on comfort and support.

- Discussing the primary goals of hospice care, including pain management and emotional well-being.

- Emphasizing that hospice care is tailored to the individual's preferences and can take place at home or in a hospice facility.

Eligibility and Decision-Making

- Explaining eligibility criteria for hospice care, typically based on a prognosis of six months or less.

- Encouraging open discussions with healthcare providers and the individual facing cancer about the decision to transition to hospice care.

- Providing information on the flexibility of hospice care, allowing individuals to return to curative treatments if their condition improves.

Collaboration with Healthcare Professionals

Communication with Healthcare Providers

● Stressing the importance of clear communication with healthcare providers about the individual's preferences.

● Encouraging dads to actively participate in discussions about transitioning to palliative or hospice care.

● Collaborating with healthcare professionals to create a care plan aligned with the individual's goals.

Involvement of Supportive Services

● Exploring the role of supportive services within palliative and hospice care, such as counseling and spiritual guidance.

● Understanding the value of a multidisciplinary team that addresses the diverse needs of the individual and the family.

● Navigating available resources and support networks.

Goals:

● Define palliative care and its role in enhancing the quality of life.

● Explain hospice care as compassionate end-of-life care and discuss its eligibility criteria.

● Encourage open communication with healthcare providers about the decision to transition to palliative or hospice care.

● Emphasize the importance of a multidisciplinary approach in addressing physical, emotional, and spiritual needs during end-of-life care.

Making Difficult Decisions

NAVIGATING DIFFICULT decisions during the end-of-life phase is an emotional and challenging process. This section provides guidance for dads facing tough choices, emphasizing communication, shared decision-making, and the importance of aligning decisions with the individual's values and wishes.

Shared Decision-Making Process

Inclusive Family Discussions

● Encouraging open and inclusive discussions within the family about difficult decisions.

● Facilitating an environment where each family member can express their thoughts and concerns.

● Emphasizing the importance of collective decision-making while respecting individual perspectives.

Involving Healthcare Professionals

● Seeking guidance from healthcare professionals who can provide insights into the medical aspects of the decision.

● Arranging family meetings with healthcare providers to discuss treatment options, potential outcomes, and the individual's preferences.

● Collaborating with medical experts to make informed decisions that align with the individual's overall well-being.

Aligning Decisions with Values and Wishes

Reflecting on Personal Values

● Guiding dads in reflecting on their personal values and beliefs.

● Encouraging consideration of how these values may influence decision-making.

● Emphasizing the significance of aligning decisions with the family's shared values.

Respecting Individual Wishes

● Emphasizing the importance of respecting the individual's wishes and autonomy.

● Discussing and documenting the individual's preferences regarding end-of-life care.

● Recognizing that decisions should be guided by what the individual deems as most meaningful and aligned with their values.

Emotional Support and Coping

Accessing Emotional Support

● Acknowledging the emotional toll of difficult decisions and providing avenues for emotional support.

● Encouraging dads to seek support from friends, family, or professional counselors.

● Creating a supportive environment that fosters open communication about feelings and concerns.

Coping Strategies for Decision-Making

● Introducing coping strategies to manage stress and emotions during the decision-making process.

● Identifying healthy outlets for expressing emotions, such as journaling or engaging in calming activities.

● Emphasizing the importance of self-care as a means of maintaining emotional well-being.

Resolving Conflict and Finding Resolution

Facilitating Open Communication

● Providing guidance on effective communication techniques to resolve conflicts within the family.

● Encouraging active listening, empathy, and the expression of concerns in a constructive manner.

● Facilitating family meetings where conflicts can be addressed openly and respectfully.

Seeking Mediation or Counseling

● Recognizing situations where external mediation or counseling may be beneficial.

● Exploring the option of involving a neutral third party to assist in resolving conflicts.

● Emphasizing the common goal of making decisions that prioritize the well-being of the individual facing cancer.

Goals:

● Promote shared decision-making within the family.

● Encourage alignment of decisions with personal values and the individual's wishes.

● Provide guidance on accessing emotional support during the decision-making process.

● Offer strategies for resolving conflicts and finding resolution in difficult decisions.

Chapter 9: After the Journey

The conclusion of the cancer journey marks a new phase for dads and their families. This chapter addresses the period following the challenges of the journey, focusing on reflection, coping with loss, and finding a path forward.

Reflection and Healing

Taking Time for Reflection

- Encouraging dads to take time for personal reflection on the entire cancer journey.

- Recognizing and acknowledging the emotions associated with the challenges faced.

- Utilizing reflective practices, such as journaling or meditation, to process thoughts and feelings.

Seeking Professional Support

- Discussing the option of seeking professional counseling or therapy for emotional healing.

- Providing information on support groups and resources designed for individuals who have completed the cancer journey.

- Emphasizing the value of seeking support as a positive step towards emotional well-being.

Coping with Loss and Grief

Understanding the Grief Process

- Acknowledging the various stages of grief that may accompany the loss of a loved one.

● Providing information on common emotional responses and coping mechanisms.

● Emphasizing the individual nature of the grief process and the importance of self-compassion.

Honoring and Remembering

● Discussing ways to honor and remember the individual who faced cancer.

● Encouraging the creation of meaningful rituals or memorial activities.

● Emphasizing the significance of preserving positive memories and celebrating the impact the individual had on the family.

REBUILDING AND MOVING Forward

Establishing New Routines

● Recognizing the need for adjustments in daily routines and family dynamics.

● Providing tips on establishing new routines that support the family's well-being.

● Emphasizing the importance of flexibility and adaptation during this transition.

Setting Personal and Family Goals

● Guiding dads in setting personal and family goals for the future.

● Encouraging a forward-looking perspective that incorporates lessons learned from the cancer journey.

● Identifying areas of growth and potential positive changes in various aspects of life.

Connecting with Others

Engaging in Community and Support Networks

● Encouraging ongoing participation in community and support networks.

● Fostering connections with others who have experienced similar journeys.

● Emphasizing the mutual support and understanding found in shared experiences.

Contributing to Advocacy and Awareness

● Discussing the potential for dads to contribute to cancer advocacy and awareness.

● Exploring opportunities to share their experiences to support others facing similar challenges.

● Emphasizing the positive impact of community engagement and giving back.

Goals:

● Guide dads in the process of reflection and emotional healing after the cancer journey.

● Provide support for coping with loss and grief, emphasizing individualized approaches.

● Offer guidance on rebuilding and moving forward, setting goals for the future.

● Encourage ongoing connections with community and support networks.

Grieving and Moving Forward

GRIEVING IS A NATURAL and individual process that accompanies the loss experienced after a cancer journey. This section offers guidance for dads on navigating the grieving process and finding ways to move forward towards healing and growth.

UNDERSTANDING THE GRIEF Process

Acknowledging Emotions

● Encouraging dads to acknowledge and express the range of emotions associated with grief, including sadness, anger, and confusion.

● Emphasizing that the grieving process is unique to each individual and may unfold at different paces.

Seeking Support

● Highlighting the importance of seeking support from friends, family, or support groups during the grieving process.

● Providing information on professional counseling or therapy as valuable resources for coping with grief.

Honoring and Remembering

Creating Memorial Rituals

● Encouraging dads to create memorial rituals or ceremonies that honor and celebrate the life of the individual who faced cancer.

● Suggesting activities such as lighting candles, planting a memorial garden, or organizing a commemorative event.

PRESERVING MEMORIES

● Providing suggestions on preserving memories, such as creating a memorial scrapbook or digital photo album.

● Discussing the positive impact of sharing stories and reminiscing about special moments with family and friends.

EMBRACING SUPPORT NETWORKS

Participating in Grief Support Groups

● Recommending participation in grief support groups where individuals can share their experiences and emotions with others who have faced similar losses.

● Emphasizing the healing power of connecting with those who understand the challenges of grieving.

Seeking Individual and Family Support

● Recognizing the value of individual and family support during the grieving process.

● Encouraging open communication within the family about their grief experiences and ways to support one another.

Finding Meaning and Growth

Reflecting on Lessons Learned

● Guiding dads in reflecting on the lessons learned from the cancer journey and the impact it had on their lives.

● Encouraging the identification of personal growth and resilience that emerged from the challenges faced.

Setting New Intentions

● Encouraging the setting of new intentions and goals for the future.

● Emphasizing the importance of focusing on positive aspirations and incorporating lessons learned from the grieving process.

Goals:

● Support dads in understanding and navigating the grief process.

● Provide guidance on honoring and remembering the individual who faced cancer.

● Encourage engagement with grief support networks for emotional healing.

● Empower dads to find meaning and growth in the aftermath of the loss.

Chapter 10: Continuing Support for Dads

The journey through cancer and loss is ongoing, and ongoing support is crucial for dads as they navigate the complexities of grief and rebuilding. This chapter provides guidance on accessing ongoing support networks, self-care strategies, and avenues for personal growth.

Engaging with Ongoing Support Networks

Participation in Bereavement Support Groups

- Encouraging ongoing participation in bereavement support groups.

- Highlighting the benefits of connecting with others who share similar experiences.

- Providing resources for finding local or online support groups.

Seeking Professional Counseling

- Discussing the option of continuing professional counseling or therapy.

- Emphasizing the value of ongoing emotional support from trained professionals.

- Providing guidance on finding therapists specializing in grief and loss.

Focusing on Self-Care

Prioritizing Physical Well-Being

- Encouraging dads to prioritize physical health through regular exercise and balanced nutrition.

- Recognizing the connection between physical well-being and emotional resilience.

- Offering practical tips for incorporating physical activity into daily routines.

Nurturing Emotional Well-Being

● Providing strategies for managing stress and cultivating emotional well-being.

● Encouraging the practice of mindfulness, meditation, or other relaxation techniques.

● Emphasizing the importance of seeking joy and finding moments of positivity.

Personal Growth and Learning

Exploring New Hobbies and Interests

● Encouraging dads to explore new hobbies or interests as a means of personal growth.

● Discussing the therapeutic benefits of engaging in creative or fulfilling activities.

● Providing resources for discovering local clubs or classes.

Continuing Education and Development

● Emphasizing the value of continuing education and skill development.

● Providing information on online courses, workshops, or community college classes.

● Encouraging dads to set personal goals for continuous learning.

Navigating Relationships and Rebuilding Connections

Communicating with Family and Friends

● Emphasizing open communication with family and friends about ongoing needs and challenges.

● Encouraging the expression of feelings and the fostering of supportive connections.

● Providing guidance on navigating evolving relationships with sensitivity.

Exploring New Social Opportunities

● Encouraging dads to explore new social opportunities for connection.

● Suggesting participation in community events, clubs, or volunteering.

● Emphasizing the potential for building meaningful connections beyond previous social circles.

Goals:

● Guide dads in accessing ongoing support through bereavement groups and counseling.

● Provide practical strategies for prioritizing physical and emotional well-being.

● Encourage personal growth through exploring new interests and continuous learning.

● Support dads in navigating relationships and rebuilding connections.

Resources for Dads Navigating the Cancer Journey

NAVIGATING THE CANCER journey as a dad involves accessing various resources that provide information, support, and assistance. Here is a compiled list of resources covering different aspects of the journey:

Cancer Information and Support:

● American Cancer Society (ACS): Website[1]

● National Cancer Institute (NCI): Website[2]

● CancerCare: Website[3]

Support for Dads and Families:

---

1. https://www.cancer.org/

2. https://www.cancer.gov/

3. https://www.cancercare.org/

- Dad's Cancer Support Group: Website

- Family Caregiver Alliance: Website[4]

- National Alliance for Caregiving: Website[5]

Emotional Support and Counseling:

- GriefShare: Website[6]

- Psychology Today (Find a Therapist): Website[7]

Health and Well-Being:

- Mayo Clinic - Coping with Cancer: Website

- American Institute for Cancer Research (AICR): Website[8]

Financial and Legal Assistance:

- Cancer Financial Assistance Coalition (CFAC): Website[9]

- LegalZoom - Estate Planning: Website[10]

End-of-Life and Bereavement Support:

- National Hospice and Palliative Care Organization (NHPCO): Website[11]

- The Compassionate Friends (Grief Support): Website[12]

---

4. https://www.caregiver.org/

5. https://www.caregiving.org/

6. https://www.griefshare.org/

7. https://www.psychologytoday.com/

8. https://www.aicr.org/

9. https://www.cancerfac.org/

10. https://www.legalzoom.com/

11. https://www.nhpco.org/

12. https://www.compassionatefriends.org/

Online Communities and Forums:

- Cancer Survivors Network: Website

- Reddit - Cancer Support: Subreddit

Caregiver and Dad-Specific Resources:

- National At-Home Dad Network: Website[13]

- Caregiver Action Network: Website[14]

Books for Dads Facing Cancer:

- "The Ultimate Guide for Dads-to-Be" by Armin Brott

- "The Cancer-Fighting Kitchen" by Rebecca Katz and Mat Edelson

- "The Emperor of All Maladies" by Siddhartha Mukherjee

Local Support Services:

- Check with local hospitals, community centers, and religious organizations for support groups, counseling services, and community events.

Glossary of Terms

BIOPSY: A MEDICAL PROCEDURE to remove a small sample of tissue for examination, usually to diagnose or determine the extent of cancer.

Chemotherapy: Treatment that uses drugs to stop the growth of cancer cells, either by killing them or inhibiting their division.

Counseling: Professional guidance and support to address emotional, psychological, or relational challenges, often provided by licensed therapists or counselors.

---

13. https://www.athomedad.org/

14. https://caregiveraction.org/

Hospice Care: Specialized care that focuses on providing comfort and support to individuals with life-limiting illnesses and their families, often in the final months of life.

Palliative Care: Specialized medical care that focuses on relieving symptoms and improving the quality of life for individuals facing serious illnesses, not limited to end-of-life care.

Prognosis: A prediction of the likely course and outcome of a medical condition, including the chance of recovery.

Radiation Therapy: Treatment that uses high doses of radiation to kill or damage cancer cells, preventing their ability to grow and divide.

Remission: A period during the cancer journey when there is a reduction or disappearance of signs and symptoms, indicating a response to treatment.

Support Groups: Gatherings of individuals facing similar challenges, providing a platform for sharing experiences, emotions, and coping strategies.

Terminal Illness: An incurable medical condition that is expected to result in the individual's death within a specific period.

Advance Care Planning: Process of making decisions about the type of medical care an individual would want to receive if they become unable to speak for themselves.

Bereavement: The state of mourning or grieving over the death of a loved one.

Resilience: The ability to adapt and bounce back in the face of adversity, demonstrating strength and coping skills during challenging times.

Grief: The emotional response to loss, encompassing a range of feelings such as sadness, anger, and acceptance.

Advocacy: The act of supporting or promoting the interests and well-being of individuals, often related to healthcare or social issues.

End-of-Life Care: Comprehensive care provided to individuals nearing the end of their life, focusing on comfort, quality of life, and support for both the individual and their family.

Grieving Process: The series of emotional and psychological stages experienced in response to a significant loss, often described as stages of denial, anger, bargaining, depression, and acceptance.

Multidisciplinary Team: A group of professionals from different disciplines (such as medicine, nursing, counseling) working collaboratively to address the various aspects of an individual's care.

Legacy Planning: The process of intentionally leaving behind a meaningful and lasting impact, often involving the creation of legacies through memories, values, or contributions.

Hope: A positive and optimistic mindset that looks forward to positive outcomes, even in the face of challenges.

Don't miss out!

Visit the website below and you can sign up to receive emails whenever DNT Publishing publishes a new book. There's no charge and no obligation.

https://books2read.com/r/B-A-VPQCB-HOMTC

BOOKS 2 READ

Connecting independent readers to independent writers.

Also by DNT Publishing

A Dad's Guide to Navigating Parenthood in a Digital Age
Buzzing Beginnings: A Beginner's Guide to Beekeeping
Courageous Compassion: Navigating Cancer as a Father.
Dip, Drizzle, Delight: The Ultimate Sauce and Marinade Handbook
The Digital Parent Playbook: Strategies for Moms
The Toddler Parenting Guide
Unveiling Strength: A Compassionate Guide Through the Cancer Journey for Moms
Navigating ADHD: Understanding, Coping, and Thriving
Unlock the Power of Love A Guide to Building Lasting Connection and Romance
Irish Delights: St. Patrick's Day Cookbook Authentic Recipes and Irish Traditions

www.ingramcontent.com/pod-product-compliance
Lightning Source LLC
Chambersburg PA
CBHW061710130726
47996CB00006B/2250